MW01089384

Transcribed by:
April Smiley

SATAN'S U-TURNS: HOW I GOT LOST WHILE GOD WAS DRIVING

MOCY PUBLISHING
WWW.MOCYPUBLISHING.COM

Detroit, Michigan

Satan's U-Turns: How I Got Lost While God Was Driving

ISBN 978-1-940831-01-5
Copyright © 2013 by Flex Stevens

Published by Mocy Publishing, LLC.
Website: www.mocypublishing.com
Email: info@mocypublishing.com
Phone: (313) 436-6944

CONTENTS

ACKNOWLEDGEMENTS

I thank God for giving me the desire to reach those around the world and to share the news that God loves us so much.

I also want to thank Pastor Tim Lambert for helping me birth my story Satan's U-Turns, God used you Tim to give me hope and to point me in the direction towards Jesus Christ.

And for my friend and brother D. Casino Bailey. You really threw a lifeline my way. I am so proud of what you have become. God's hand is on you.

And for Brother Simmons "Delivered" for taking the time to help me mold this book together, your guidance and prayers have blessed me dearly.

CHRIST–4–LIFE
Dana 'Flex' Stevens 228599

INTRODUCTION

I was told when I was seven years old, by my mother, that the devil was inside of me and that there was something wrong with me. That just stuck in my mind while I was growing up. I don't know why, but I just believed that I was a mistake and that God didn't want to have anything to do with me. After all, if the devil was taking up residence in my soul, why would God want anything to do with me? Maybe that's why I got picked on, bullied, ignored, etc.

I thought it was all God's fault. Maybe you feel the same way. If so, this book is for you. It's our bad choices that pull us away from even wanting to think about God. From prostitution to drug use, from abortion to alcoholism, from telling big lies to telling half truths, from cussing to gambling, from having pre-marital fornication to having an after marriage adulterous affair, from intentionally hurting people to accidentally killing someone, or to intentionally killing someone; keep in mind that whatever it may be that haunts you within the recesses of your mind, or makes you feel weighed down with guilt and shame, you need to know this truth...
GOD IS IN LOVE WITH YOU!!

Before I gave my life over to the Lord and Saviour Jesus Christ, I had no idea that my life and everything I went through was a war between God and Satan for my soul. We know that God is all powerful and that our enemy "the Devil", is of second-rate power. Being that God allows us the liberty to choose for ourselves what road to take, Satan will begin the battle by presenting so many roads and u-turns in our way that we get lost before we get started. But God in his omnipotent way always has a plan to draw our attention to the cross. A sign that will take any satanic u-turn and straighten it out and put us in the right direction.

For me, it took 33 years of u-turns that would not quit. As you read this book, use it to learn and understand how Satan tries to not only get a foothold in our lives, but how he will use this leverage to get us to make a u-turn away from God's road.

As I sit here in this prison cell writing this book, I hear the voice of my Saviour guiding me, by His Spirit, on what I am to tell you. Yeah, I said He's guiding me, the once upon a time street dealer and hit man for hire. But now I'm a man forgiven by the Love and Grace of God that comes only through His Son, Our Lord Jesus Christ. Now that's Love. Believe it or not, God want to give that love to you as well, you just have to receive it.

Chapter 1

The Battle of Rejection

And whosoever shall not receive you, nor hear your words, when ye depart out of that house or city, shake off the dust of your feet.

Matthew 10:14

Although I was too young to remember the actions that took place between my birth mother and I, the dust of negativity and rejection stuck to the bottom of my feet as Social Services came and took me away. I was an 18-month-old infant when my right leg and skull were fractured because of the affects of child abuse and abandonment from this unknown woman.

The adoption files read that she was a drug user and a paranoid schizophrenic. My biological father is unknown.

I was too young to remember all of these things, the only thing I do remember is seeing my adopted mother's face as she looked at me as if she won a prize at a game show. Her name was Ethel Marie Stevens. She was the mother of 4 children, now 5 as I was the first and last adopted into her family.

It's sad that children can often detect negative vibes from certain people very easily. From the absence of their presence and the looks on their faces when they were present, I knew that my mother's children did not approve of my adoption.

People who feel like outcasts, people who have been through so much pain become a prime target for the devil to work on their thoughts. It's easy for him to do this when you're young.

Rejection causes one to rebel or to bring the attention that one feels they are being robbed of. Where does this idea come from? I honestly believe that Satan is a part of it. When you lock a child in a room for hours at a time, what you are doing is allowing the Devil to become the child's imaginary friend. If you're asking where God was during all this, just look at the bigger picture. God pulled me out of my birth mother's oppression and into a secure house of food, shelter, and love. Always remember that where there is a small screen of satanic warfare there is a big picture of God's sovereignty governing everything. He brought me from an abusive mother to a foster mother who did love me, but yet she had issues of her own, and her issues affected everyone living in this new home I was adopted into. My foster father, now he was another story. He was my best friend. He was the "H" in humble. He lived for everyone but himself. Everyone's needs came first and he provided for them all. He never showed anger. He always spoke with a soft voice. Well, that was up until I got much older which you will read later on as the story gets deeper.

While everyone else gave me the rejected cold shoulder, my father, Lester, was always there. He took me places, played games with me. To this very day I can still remember him taking me into my bedroom with the blue painted walls with pictures of circus clowns everywhere. He would sit down and read stories to me from my Walt Disney books, or he would teach me how to say my prayers, "Now I lay me down to sleep. I pray the lord my soul to keep. If I should die before I wake, I pray the Lord my soul to take."

I used to think that Satan took control of my mother to take her anger out on me and God used my father to let me know that someone loved me. It was rejection and love tag teaming in my life.

As time went on, I got older, the contention grew in my heart. I don't think she knew how angry I was at her. She became sick and was prescribed so much medication that her bedroom looked like a pharmacy. A part of me knew that it was her illness that caused her to be so irate and self-centered. But the satanic arrows were implying in my thoughts that she only adopted me so that I would be her stress reliever, her slap-around tool when she was angry; her butler and maid when she wanted to boss someone around. Then, after all that, she would do something nice for me, like buy me a toy, or take me shopping. But she would make sure that I remembered she did such a nice thing and how she went out of her way to do it even though I didn't deserve it.

When I became a teenager, I started rejecting. It was

my way of putting some points on the scoreboard. It made me feel like a winner to look my mother in the face on my 16th birthday and say, "Please, don't make me a birthday cake, and don't give me any gifts." It made me feel triumphant to look at her older children, who never spoke to me from the day I arrived, and finally express my feelings and say, "I don't care, I know you all hate me, I don't care much for any of you either."

Why did I feel this way, and what took me so long to express my emotions? I personally feel that by accepting something for so long, you wind up becoming it – the
rejectee becomes the rejector.

So many times I have dusted my feet off and ran out of that house and hunted for those who would accept me, embrace me, and make me feel as though I belonged. I didn't get much of that from the house that I was imprisoned in. Oh, it was always there, I just didn't get it. If you don't get it then it will be hard to notice that it's even there. I guess Satan forgot to tell me that she was very sick. I guess Satan forgot to tell me to embrace my father more when I was thinking about negativity toward my mother. I guess Satan forgot to tell me to cry out and let my mother's children know that I needed a few friends. I guess Satan forgot to tell me to pray and listen to God so that I would see the things God was trying to show me.

Chapter 2

The Battle for Acceptance

When Jesus therefore saw his mother, and the disciple standing by, whom he loved, he saith unto his mother, woman, behold thy son! Then saith he to the disciple, Behold thy mother! And from that hour that disciple took her unto his own home.

John 19:26-27

Don't we wish it were that easy? One command from God and we accept each other as family. Everyone has been found guilty within their own hearts of seeking acceptance from others it's a natural. How you go about it is a different story. We can do it God's way, or we can do it our way which leaves a door open in our minds for the Devil to enter with suggestive ideas.

Because I lost the battle of rejection, my attention became directed toward acceptance through the streets that I ran to after running from home. What's in the streets? Drugs, money, women, materialistic living, reputations, glory from people, everything I thought I wanted but nothing God was trying to give me.

A known drug dealer out of my area of Detroit somehow made me feel important and respected as he employed me to be a drug pusher for what I was told was now "our" crew. Finally! I had become a part of something, I belonged, and he even gave me a gun and a place to stay. He must have cared about my welfare or he wouldn't have given me the gun, right? Little did I know back then that it wasn't me he worried about, it was the worry of someone taking his money and drugs from me that was more important. Satan knows that with drugs, money, and guns, murder is not far behind, but he won't let you know that. In fact, you become so blinded by the acceptance and all the attention that everything else becomes unimportant.

When you're on your own and you don't have an adult yelling at you and giving you orders, you being to feel important, you have friends now, and you meet new friends throughout the day. You're making all this money, but you're giving most of it back to the guy you're selling drugs for. But it's okay because Satan tells you that you will soon be the one in charge, that you're just getting your feet wet so that you will soon be the number one dealer.

But Satan forgot to tell me what it would cost me to do so. He failed to let me know how I would become the leader of street crime. Before I could even focus on how or when, I wound up with all these different beautiful women throwing themselves at me, telling me they wanted to be in my life. The acceptance game just got better (so I thought). When the money was gone and fame is gone, so are they. When your heart is broken you can somehow hear God speak.

Something told me to just go back home one day while my drug dealing boss kept asking me too many questions about where my loyalty was with him. Every time I returned home my mother and father would gladly accept me back. Notice how I wrote "every time I returned." It was there the whole time – acceptance.

I honestly feel that Satan directed my attention to the streets so I would not find what was already at home. True acceptance. The sad part is that I kept running to the streets. The world is an addiction within itself. This is why so many people can't stay at home and sit down when they're young. They have to keep going out, but as one gets up in age they would rather stay in. They have seen and done it all already. They have nothing to prove nor gain. Acceptance is buying the flashy car so everyone will see you, or wearing the most jewelry so not only will you be seen, but you show that you can afford it. It's blasting your music out of your car so that everyone will hear you and not the music itself. Going to clubs and bars with the fellas and drug hustlers is so that the world will know that you are accepted by what seems to be important. This type of acceptance brings envy and strife from those who are seeking the acceptance they think you seem to have. But Satan won't tell you this. Although, he is behind it.

Chapter 3

One Fall Becomes God's Call

But ye are a chosen generation, a royal priesthood, an holy nation, a peculiar people; that ye should shew forth the praises of him who hath called you out of darkness into his marvelous light;

I Peter 2:9

Selling drugs caught the attention of money hungry women, other drug dealers, and the police as well. I was going back and forth from Detroit, MI to Port Huron, MI on a day to day basis selling drugs and opening new drug houses. Drug dealers from Port Huron did not like the fact that a guy from Detroit was coming on their "turf" selling dope and robbing them of their clientele. The Port Huron police caught wind of this situation and they set up a drug bust during my attempt to open a drug house in a new area of their city. Two days after I had the drug house running, the task force officers busted the house. As I tried to flee from the back door of the house, I was shot in the hip by an undercover police officer with a 357 bullet that knocked me clear across the backyard area of the home.

After two days of unconsciousness, I woke up in a hospital bed with two Port Huron police officers guarding my room door and a doctor standing over me asking how I felt.

He explained to me that I came close to dying, but the only thing that was on my mind was how my mother and father were going to act when they found out about me selling drugs and now in trouble with the law. I had no idea that my mother and father were already at the hospital waiting to see me when I gained consciousness. When they were finally able to come in and see me, I thought of a quick lie to justify what happened.

"Mom I was at the wrong place at the wrong time." That's all I could think of on such short notice. As always, my mom would believe almost anything I would say when it came to anyone outside the Stevens family blaming me for anything.

After thirty days of hospital care and rehabilitation of my hip, I was transferred to the county jail where I stayed for three months awaiting my trial and sentence. During this time I met a man who was also awaiting trial for a murder case he was involved in. his name was Joseph, and all he did in his cell was pray and read his Bible. He also worked out frequently on the exercise bars and in the workout area of the recreation room.

I began to start exercising to build up my strength and renew my physical agility. Joseph and I began talking quite a bit during our workout session, and he would do everything he could to introduce me to the biblical teachings. But I was not interested in the Bible or God at all. He gave me a small Bible to keep in my cell. One night I had trouble getting to sleep so I grabbed the

Bible off my desk and began reading the gospel of Matthew. By the time I got to chapter 27:27-31, I was in tears.

The next day I walked in Joseph's cell and I told him what I felt while reading the book of Matthew. We both got on our knees together and we prayed a sinner's prayer and I then accepted Jesus Christ as My Lord and Saviour.

For some reason I felt as though a huge weight was lifted off my shoulders. I even gave my worry of the upcoming drug case sentencing to God. I prayed to God to give me another chance and to release me from the jail with only the punishment of probation.

Thirty days later I was sent to court from my cell to see the Judge.

It all happened so fast that I don't remember what the Judge said. All I remember was hearing the words "probation," and "Don't let me see you in my court again!"

My first answered prayer! But at the same time, Satan was whispering in my ear, "That was only luck." Either way, I was just happy to get out of that jail, go back home, and put this whole thing behind me. But by doing that, I would have to also put something else in front of me. I needed a new goal and focus in my life.

It's funny how exercise and recovery from a gunshot

would transformed my physique from a frame of alcohol and drinking and fast food, to a frame of muscularity and a promising career in the world of body building. I gave God my word that I would no longer sell drugs or live a life of crime. My focus was to stick to my word to the God that died on a cross for my sins.

I went job hunting. I started going to church on Sundays with my Aunt Jenny. Aunt Jenny was actually my best friend's guardian. I was so close to their family that I called her my Aunt Jenny. She knew I had a past of street crime and drug dealing. She never judged, she just wanted me to go to church with her. Little did I know this was a part of God's call for my life. I truly believe that God was trying to transform me into what He wanted me to be.

As time went on, my life began to change. I was lifting weights with well known bodybuilders. I was entering into contests and guest posing shows. Everywhere I went I was recognized as the new up and coming pro bodybuilder that would represent Michigan.

At the same time I took time out to help kids that were going through problems and needed direction in their lives. There's something that happens inside of me when it comes to kids. Especially kids that are going through rough situations. I guess what we relate to the most is what we help give others a hand to help conquer.

While doing these things I was also working. Bodybuilding is a 24-7 job itself, but I was also working at a chicken fast-food restaurant, and I worked at night running security at a nightclub.

One day, I went to the church on a Tuesday afternoon because the preacher wanted to have a meeting with me in his office. He sat me down and said that he saw something in me. He wanted me to get baptized and he asked me if I could come to church on special meeting days so I could be more a part of the church family. This felt too much like commitment for me. I did not want to be a part of anything. I just wanted to do right by God and live my own life. I did not want to say this to the preacher, so I just said to him, "Let me think about it, give me some time, maybe later." I left his office and never came back to church again.

I missed the call.

Chapter 4

Driving with the Lights Off

They soon forgot his works; they waited not for his counsel:

Psalm 106:13

Dedicating to the church program was not in my schedule, nor was it my focus. I wanted to be the popular muscle-man, I wanted to make money, I wanted to be successful, and I wanted to do it my way, not the preacher's. Little did I know, God was using the preacher, the church members, and Aunt Jenny to show me the way God wanted to lead my path, instead of my way in my own understanding.

If you don't follow the right path you're going to wind up where you don't want to be. Why do people get so irate after they realize they are on the wrong road? Because they know that they have to stay on that wrong road until they can find a way to get off. The only way to go back to God's road is to simply go back into focus on God and God alone. When I declined his will for me, I opened up a window for Satan to suggest my next move.

One day while on my way back from work, I ran into an old friend who was a known drug dealer and street hustler. He jumped out of a red BMW. He had what seemed to look like a supermodel girlfriend sitting in his car. I can still remember what he said to me as he approached me, "what's up big guy? I see you're a muscle guy now working a 9 to 5. I guess you don't want to live the good life anymore." He then said, "If you need anything, and if you're ready to get rich again, come by my house later." I declined his offer because his girlfriend was staring right at me, and I didn't want to seem desperate. But in my heart I envied his success.

Throughout that day he was on my mind. I don't know why I couldn't shake his offer out of my mind. I didn't want to go back into the drug dealing world. I guess I just needed the acceptance (recognition). "Something" (meaning Satan) kept suggesting to me that I should dip into the drug trade just to make enough money to live comfortable. This way I didn't have to waste my time at a job cooking chicken at a fast-food joint.

"Something" also kept saying that a few deals here, a few deals there, and I'll be financially on track and it will hold me until my first big pay off muscle show.

"Something" also said that there will be no risk at all if I employ people to do my drug runs and dirty work. I embraced "my own understanding" which was nothing more than what Satan was telling me.

I quit my job, I made deals with this known drug dealer, I met and employed guys to help me make money and my career slowly faded. First I didn't have time in my schedule for the preacher and the church family. Now, I didn't have time for the Powerhouse Gym and my career. I would pop into the gym at least once or twice a week because I missed it so much. When one has a career in sports it becomes a part of them that they can never let go. The uncomfortable part was walking into a gym or fitness center and being recognized and disapproved of at the same time. When your focus changes, others will notice it by the way you live and carry yourself. When you pull up in the gym parking lot in a shiny sports car, wearing diamonds on your hands and neck, people will question your lifestyle.

I remember being in the gym locker room and a well known bodybuilder walked in and noticed my gun in my waist that I thought my unzipped jacket was concealing. He gave me a look that said, "I used to respect you." To hide the hurtful feeling I had, I began to brag of the money I was bringing in, and the club I was buying, and how important I was. It was my way of taking the sting out of my own backslidden actions.

I can't believe that I would actually get mad at good people for being upset that I was making the wrong choices that were killing not only my career but also my relationships with the people who tried to help me and open the right doors to the sport of bodybuilding in my life. I didn't know who I was anymore. I went from protein shakes to beer and gin on a daily basis. I had to drink in order to ignore the truth of how I really felt about myself. It was hard to do at first because I hated the smell and taste of alcohol. But all the hustlers and gangsters drank. So I had to follow the trend to fit in.

Plus, I got tired of all the health jokes the fellas kept shooting at me.

Little did I know that soon everyone would be shooting at me. But not with friendly jokes next time it would be with real bullets.

I never thought you can be loved and hated at the same time by the same group of people. I think it's like they love to use you but they hate the fact that they won't always be able to use you. That's how it is in street life, but most people won't figure this out until after it explodes in their life. It wasn't like this when I worked at the fast-food joint. I was never paranoid with alcohol on my breath when I spent hours and hours working in the gym. Nobody was looking down on me when I went to church. If only I had stayed in the car God was driving instead of jumping in a car with no lights.

Chapter 5

The Road Trip of Pride

Therefore hear now this, thou that art given to pleasures, that dwellest carelessly, that sayest in thine heart, I am, and none else beside me; I shall not sit as a widow, neither shall I know the loss of children.

Isaiah 47:8

When you're not focused on God you have nowhere to gain inner strength from. So, you substitute by using self-encouragement. The most dangerous part about self-encouragement is that it becomes all about you. You wind up taking all the credit for everything you accomplish or what you think you have accomplished, and like cancer, self-sufficiency, self-encouragement, self-centeredness all lead to self-destruction. But Satan won't tell you these things. He will only tell you that "You don't need anyone, you can do it yourself, only trust you, you come before anyone, and, show everyone that you're the boss."

Street life is a competition within itself. You have to have the best looking car on the street. You have to have the most glamorous jewelry and clothes. You have to be known and respected by everyone, and everyone has to respect and fear you at the same time.

Satan won't tell you that to make these things happen you will have to hurt people, scare people, and even kill people. By this time during many wrong turns I no longer cared about the feelings of others. It was all about me and those who showed loyalty to me.

I remember a few times my guilt would kick in when nobody was around, and I would look up and whisper to God, "I know you hate me, I know I let you down, I'm just gonna hate you back, this way we have something in common."

I essentially put God and my birth mother in the same category, they both knew me when I was born into this world of sin, and they both ignored me. I don't know what made me think this way. Maybe it was the drinking and marijuana use. Maybe it was because I got caught up in such a hateful world that I convinced myself that everyone (even God) hated me.

"The best way to get back at those that hate you is to give them something to hate you for." Satan told me that, and at that time I thought it was the best advice ever. I began showing off in public places, I would actually set money on fire in front of my friends, or I would tear hundred-dollar bills up in front of people in a store line. I would threaten people on a daily basis. I got a kick out of belittling people and talking down to those who thought they were more important. I was so out of control that I exalted myself within the Stevens family.

I built my organization called "Murder One." I had so much money coming in that I filled my basement with weights and the best exercise equipment so that I could train at home and not have to worry about going to Powerhouse Gym and being an outcast to the "good and honest once-upon-a-time friends," who hated evil drug dealers.

I figured with some quick steroid use and a few months of training that I could have the best of both world – the career and the streets. Satan forgot to tell me that the steroid use would only ignite my anger more and take my pride issues to a level where even my parents would soon fear me.

I remember one morning I walked out on the front porch of my mother's home and I saw the little children across the street playing with their toys. The kids no longer looked at me when I would walk out of my front door. They used to always say "Hi" to me, and "Make a muscle!" Now they looked away when they would see me get in my car.

One time the kid next door said, "My mom told me that I can't speak to you anymore." This was shortly after my house was shot up with machine gun bullets by other enemy drug dealers. I think when that kid said those words to me, it was more painful than the time I got shot in my hip in the Port Huron drug bust. That's when I knew I was a total Loss. Now I was only waiting for my time to die and go to hell.

Out of all that was going on in my so-called life, it took that little kid's words to humble me and show me that I was once someone important but now I am less than nothing hiding behind a street reputation. I then learned that the long-term pain of that which lies is greater than the short-term pleasure of the sin that is committed. My life was full of sin, I was out of control. I put me first in everything. The more stunts I pulled, the more (in)famous I became. The women wanted me, the fellas looked up to me as if I was a celebrity (ghetto fabulous). I needed this attention to keep my pain of failure quiet. I knew how to hide my guilt too. Just keep everyone laughing at your jokes. Buy gifts for everyone around you. You never show weakness, you have all the answers, and you always brag about your accomplishments. Oh yeah, and stay drunk. Pride is very painful; it takes a lot of work to stay on the throne of high mindedness. One has to keep all eyes on them, and they will do everything in order to maintain this attention, even selling their souls to sin itself. I know what you were thinking, you're saying, 'nobody can actually sell their souls to Satan." I know this, but when you're elbow deep in self-centeredness and exaltation you will do anything to stay there.

Chapter 6

No Turning Back

Thou shall not kill. Exodus 20:13

When you're living a life full of iniquity and danger, murder will find its place. Death that comes from murder does not care who you are, what kind of reputation you have, how much money you have, or what kind of car you drive.

A famous rap music star said in an interview on MTV, "Death is serious because it ain't no coming back from it." Within six months after this interview was aired, this same famous gangster rap music star was gunned down in a drive-by shooting.

In street life we justify everything we do by whatever rules we make. "It's okay, as long as you don't get caught, it's either them or me, kill or be killed, make examples or become one," etc. if you ask me, I would tell you that it's Satan's systematic way of making one so blind to evil that they don't look at it as being wrong anymore. It's the essence of depravity.

The Bible shows a clear example of the depraved mind in Luke 23:39-40. **And one of the malefactors which were hanged railed on him, saying, If thou be Christ, save thyself and us. But the other answering rebuked him, saying, Dost not thou fear God, seeing**

thou art in the same condemnation? The criminal who ran his mouth with insults while on his way to hell was so blind with his ways that he could not even see the Son of the Living God hanging next to him.

I never thought I would ever get so lost in myself that I would kill someone and see it as only a part of the lifestyle and nothing more. But there was yet still a part of me that knew I was in deep hot water with God after a drug deal resulted in me murdering the drug supplier just to impress one of my employees. Looking a man in the eyes just before you shoot him will not make you feel like Clint Eastwood. This is no movie, there are no stunt doubles, no second screen takes, it's real, it will haunt you and the longer you think you have gotten away with it, it will drive you crazy.

Being that it was bothering me so much was a signal that I had not yet hit that stage of depravity. There was still a chance. All I had to do was run up in a church, confess my sinful living, and the turn myself in at the police station. But Satan said, "No! Don't be stupid, he was only a drug dealer, the world wanted him dead anyway. It happens all the time. It's not as bad as it looks. Besides, God gave up on you shortly after you were born, so stop worrying about God!" Satan would not stop talking. He kept suggesting that I should just take my gun out my shoulder holster and go to a quiet place, park my car, and blow my brains out. This way all the stress would no longer be on my mind. I kept thinking about my mind being all over the car seats and dash board after the bullet did its job. Then keeping the stress just seemed to be a better choice.

But it left a door in my decision making. Now I felt as though I could kill anyone that got in my way and that I would always get away with it. After all, it's organized crime and these things happen. I tried to deceive myself in believing that, but I could not shake the fact that I was clearly on my way to hell for sure. Maybe there is no Jesus Christ. What if the Bible is nothing more than a lie? Maybe we all keep dying and coming back over and over until we get it right. What if there's no such thing as heaven. What if, what if, what if... all my what if thoughts could not escape the question "What now?"

Chapter 7

The Fall That Ended it All

The way of the wicked is as darkness: They know not at what they stumble.

Proverbs 4:19

It's 2:00 am and it's raining. I'm sitting in the back of a police car. These handcuffs are very tight. There are police cars everywhere in the area of the crime scene. I got caught right on the spot. A strong box filled with a large sum of money in one hand and a 9mm handgun in the other. Little did I know the house I was in was surrounded by police. If I would have known this I would not have killed the owner of the house.

Satan did not let me know that the police were secretly awaiting for me to come out of the house, he was too busy telling me to kill the witness, take the case of money and get back into the car.

I knew something was not right about this deal. Something told me not to make this pick up. I should have sent one of my "fall guy" employees, that way I would not be in this police car right now. What was I thinking?

I never make mistakes like this. What am I going to do? This does not look good, I'm going down for this one. Get a hold of yourself. Focus! Focus!

I'll get a good lawyer and get him or her to buy me a judge, or at least buy me a short-term jail sentence. That's what guys like us do. This is why we are "above the law."

I kept this attitude going from the time I was arrested until the day of my trial. Nothing went the way I had planned. I could not buy my way out. I could not bust my way out. The only "out" I got was shipped straight out to Jackson Prison with a life sentence. Little did I know God was there the whole time in my life waiting and waiting for me to come to him for help and change.

How did I know this? Because my first night in Jackson Prison I could hear the still small voice telling me "you still have time, turn to me and I will renew you." But I did not answer. In fact, I answered to the praise and respect I quickly gained in the prison. Your street reputation will spill into the prison system, that alone has a lot to do with why people are treated the way they are within the prison walls. As soon as I thought to go to church and Bible study, the u-turn of the prison reputation sign blinded me from God. I figured I would use my reputation as a stepping stone of my goal to break my way out of prison.

I figured it would be typical and hypocritical to think about God now. I even made up a joke; I would ask people, "Hey, did you know that God was in prison?" As soon as someone would fall into this question with a response like, "Who told you this?" I would then reply with, "That's where everyone seems to find Him."

I could not stand Christian inmates. I didn't even know why. I think it had to do with the fact that I saw something in them that I wanted but was not ready to receive because I knew I had to give up my ego, sinful mindsets, and most importantly, my agenda to get free by any means necessary. I can't do these things and kiss up to God at the same time. This goes to show you that my perception was all polluted. I could not focus on God because I was forming myself into a godlike figure. I could not hear God's call because I was too busy listening to the voices of prisoners calling me and admiring my reputation (and listening to myself).

Can you believe that our sovereign God still showed his abundant grace and waited still?

Chapter 8

False Presentation

A time to rend, and a time to sew; a time to keep silence, and a time to speak.

Ecclesiastes 3:7

Ten years into my prison term and I'm still doing the same thing, spending money on prison items, talking trash, lifting weights, and hating myself more and more. I need to do something that will make me alive again. "I know, I'll build my own gang. After all, I already have the popularity and support of 'loyal' associates, what can go wrong?"

I called this group "The Allegiance Family," a group of loyal soldiers that have the same focus, which is freedom, money, and respect. This will be my ticket to gain the power I need to get out of this prison mess and back to my street throne where I belong. I had this self-centered thought that someone was out there in the streets living the mobster life pretending to be me while I was caged up in prison.

The whole 'take over the city dream' kept popping up in my mind, but while this gang was rapidly growing, the only thing that kept popping was trouble on the prison yard, and it was all my fault. Not only was I starting wars with other gangs and Islamic groups, I was also making the Christians angry by running secret meetings in the back rows of the church services. I didn't care though, I did what I wanted to do. I got hooked on prison wine that prisoners would secretly make and sell. I also got off into taking "get high" pills, which is any type of prescription medication that an inmate would sell on the prison yard. I figured if I can't escape from prison today, at least I have a way to escape mentally.

I'm in prison surrounded by guards and rules and other inmates that I would never associate with in the real world. I hear keys jingling, cell doors slamming, voices barking orders over a unit speaker, the smell of awful food cooked in the chow hall, I hear some of the most uncivil conversations going on from cell to cell. The only way to deal with this is through a mind-altering drug that will send my thoughts on cloud nine.

Satan did not tell me that this solution would become so addictive that not only will I not want to eat anything, but that I also wouldn't be able to function without these drugs. I was being torn down inside. I kept my fronts up by cracking jokes or just remaining quiet around others. I needed to be put back together. I needed a mending that would give me a fresh start at life.

That's when it happened. One morning while listening to rap music in my cell and preparing to light a cigar and take a few get high pills, my cell door opened with a voice over the speaker telling me to report to the case manager's office.

As I entered the unit case manager's office I could feel

something bad in the air. It was bad alright; bad news from home. All I heard were the words, "Father" and "died". Everything else he said was blocked out of my hearing. I went back to my cell and got high all day on pills. I stared out of my window looking up at the sky wondering what my father was doing that very second while he was in heaven. For some reason it seemed as though there was a sale on pills that same day, because everyone kept coming to my cell with deals on drugs and I accepted them all.

I knew that God knows all, even our thoughts, so I began to think things knowing that God would hear. "God, I know you're reading my mind right now, I know you think I'm going to cry out to you, I'm not though, I'm not going to kiss up to you so take your 'all power' and find someone else to preach to. I'm not even going to open my mouth and speak. Every pill I pop is my way of saying I don't want to hear from you. You took my Dad, you took my Grandmother, you took my Mother, you took everything from me. I get it, you just wanted to take the only people in this world that cared about me so that I would live an even worse life without caring people in my life, Right? Well, guess what God Almighty, your plan did not work. I'm still standing and I'm not shedding any tears."

(Same day, the drugs are now taking full effect.)

(My thoughts now becoming whispers.) "God, why did you make me? Why do you hate me? Why did you take my Dad to heaven? You could have left him here with me. He was all I had left. He was my Dad, my only friend. Tell him I love him. Tell him I miss him already."

"I hate you God. I'm not scared of you. I never asked to be born so why should I ask you for help? Why should I do what you say to do? Where were you when my birth Mother beat me half to death? Answer that Mr. All Powerful! Where were you when I got picked on in school for no reason? Where were you when I tried to live right but had no money?"

(Now I'm drinking coffee to keep the drugs from making me drowsy and passing out.)

(My voice picks up) "Okay God, I guess I'm next. I guess you're going to put me to death too and send me to hell, right? I can help you with that Mr. Almighty, I'll kill myself with a razor right now. This way I can tell you how I feel about you face to face."

I stopped talking and grabbed a shaving razor off my desk and took the razor out of the plastic handle and sat it on my sink. I started pacing the cell floor calculating in my mind what time the officer would make his last round so I could do this suicide thing right.

The room began to spin. I started to feel sick; I could not focus on anything. Then the tears came. I fell on the bed and stared at the walls.

"What do you want me to do God" I need help, please

help me. Just tell me what you want me to do and I'll do it, okay? If I still have a chance, just let me know."

I then fell asleep.

I awoke the next morning feeling different. The last thing I needed to see was a get-high pill. After coming back from breakfast, I made myself a cup of coffee and began pacing the floor.

My mind was on my deceased father. I stopped pacing and began staring at all the posters of half-naked women that I covered my cell walls up with. 'Something' came over me and I began ripping all the posters off the walls.

Then an inmate came by my cell to say hello. I was already in the middle of some type of mind renewal when the posters came down. I looked at the inmate standing in front of my cell door and I said, "I want you to take all these girl magazines and sell them, keep them, do whatever you want with them, I just want them out of my room. I even went a step further and handed him my rap music tape collection and told him to sell them as well.

During that same day, I began telling several inmates that I was through taking pills and listening to rap music. Everyone looked at me as if I had gone crazy. The strange part is that they never gave that look when I was doing drugs; it was only when I stopped doing the things that everyone else does that I'm looked at as being crazy. It's been over a year now since that night I cried out to God. Nowadays, I just talk to my Father in heaven. He is still mending me in the way He sees fit. Only now, I'm sitting still to allow Him to complete His divine work.

It was Gods will for me to write this book. Now I see the danger signs, now I see the potholes in the road. I no longer pick up hitchhikers. I no longer stop the car and leave the doors unlocked. Satan will do anything in his power to scratch your new paint job, we are in a spiritual war. We must listen and take hold of God's voice when He's trying to keep us on the Road Less Traveled.

Chapter 9

To Be Born Again

But ye shall receive power, after that the Holy Ghost is come upon you: and ye shall be witnesses unto me both in Jerusalem, and in all Judea, and in Samaria, and unto the uttermost part of the earth.

Acts 1:8

To be "born again" means to be made "new". The Holy Spirit comes into our heart and regenerates you into what God wants you to be, and He seals you for salvation. Because of this regeneration process, my focus became more fixed on God. I needed to know everything I could of God's plan for the world and what expectation He has of me.

Through time, the more I focused on God, the less I cared about everything else in life; I began putting off my old ways and habits. Negative rap and rock music, x-rated magazines, even my words began to change and I no longer use bad language. I developed a new interest; I felt the need to buy books that would help me understand God's word more. I now see that not only will God put these types of desires in your heart, He will also provide the open doors of opportunity for you to gain everything you need to achieve his plan for your life. This is how I knew it was God's will for me to preach and win souls to Christ.

I began listening to radio preachers just to understand the Bible more, but soon I became more interested in preaching the Word while I at the same time was learning the Word. One day during my time out on the prison yard, I had a talk with an inmate friend of mine. I told him my testimony and how God had changed my life. I told him that God will do the same for him. He immediately had the desire to pray with me and accept Jesus Christ in his life. We prayed, and he got saved before the yard period was over.

After returning to my cell I realized for the first time that I could be useful. I felt as though God gave me another chance to live again but this time I had a purpose. God actually used me to save a soul! Now I can't stop. My only focus is to get close to those who don't know Christ.

Just to be prepared, I've begun studying other doctrines and false religions so that I can bring the true Word of God and boldly preach to these lost non-believers and show them the truth. I pray and work unceasingly that they will give up their false ungodly system of beliefs and come to the cross.

Jesus' aim was to connect us with God. John 10;10 says **The thief cometh not, but for to steal and to kill, and to destroy: I am come that they might have life, and that they might have it more abundantly.** For little over 30 years Satan has stolen my blessings, he has stolen the life God had planned. A few years ago I surrendered my life to Christ. Now Satan can't steal from me anymore.

Not only do I spend my days in prayer with my Father in heaven, not only do I spend time in bible study and research, not only do I fellowship with other Christians, not only do I direct my attention to those who are lost and preach Christ to them, but I am also becoming living proof that I have a Big God that can do big things.

Jeremiah 32:27 says **Behold, I am the lord, the God of all flesh: is there anything to hard for me?** God's glory comes when He does the extraordinary thing in an ordinary person like Flex Stevens. Trust me; this is only the beginning of many things to come. God told me so.

Chapter 10

The New Man

Therefore if any man be in Christ, he is a new creature: old things are passed away; behold, all things are become new.

2 Corinthians 5:17

It's such a strange thing, I can't stand negative music, I'm against drug use, I don't watch television much because there is such ungodliness on almost every channel, I can't be around people who use such foul choice words when they speak. To put it plainly, "I hate sin."

Some would say that the apostles turned the world upside down preaching Christ's resurrection. But if you ask me, I would say the world was already upside down. When you meet Christ you turn right-side-up the way you were created to be.

Why do I hate sin? Because I walk in love. Now every time I walk past people I think to myself, "Does this person know Jesus?" Now I spend my time in God's word so that I can have the helpful answers to many biblical questions that non-believers have so that they can come to Christ.

I am a true slave to the cross. I keep God in mind from the time I wake up until the time I get ready for bed.

With a mindset like this you will see all types of spiritual warfare. But, you have to know you're in a spiritual war to see it or you'll be blind. If you're blind, it's because you're on the wrong team. By walking in God's will you are walking in the light, you are walking in the spiritual kingdom of God's realm.

This enables you to preach, to lend a hand, to love, to protect yourself from sinful thoughts and to avoid sinful people, to have a strong hunger for prayer and spending time with the Father alone in a quiet place, and to learn everything there is in God's word.

This is only a mere fragment of the ongoing growth I'm experiencing as "The New Man". This is only the beginning. With Christ Jesus there is no ending.

We all make our own choices in life. The devil cannot make us do anything. Every choice we make effects the way we live, and the lives of those we come in contact with. Most importantly, we will ALL answer to every choice we make – every act, every word every thought – when our time on earth is up.

The Bible says "For all have sinned, and come short of the glory of God." Romans 3:23 The good news is that Jesus paid the price for our sin. He opened a new door: a door that frees us from the power and penalty of sin: a door of hope and of purpose. This door is open to you now if you are reading this and you have never accepted Jesus Christ as your Lord and Saviour. Romans 10:9 says "That if thou shalt confess with thy mouth the Lord

Jesus, and shalt believe in thine heart that God hath raised him from the dead, thou shalt be saved." It's that easy. Put your faith in Him and Him alone. There is no other way. God Bless. Flex Stevens #228599.

STEP ONE: Believe That God Loves You. (Yes, You!)

I remember the first birthday party I was invited to. I was eleven years old and the neighbors down the street came to my home to inform my parents that their daughter was turning twelve and that she wanted me to attend her birthday party. When my parents gave me the news, I was puzzled. I thought, "Why would she want me at her party?" Then I figured that maybe every kid in the neighborhood was invited. Maybe she just wants a lot of birthday presents; but to my surprise, when I arrived to the party, I noticed that I was the only one boy there. The room was filled with young girls. It was the middle of winter, yet I was sweating and shaking from all the eyes that were now fixed on me as I walked in the living room. The Birthday Girl was so happy to see me, she ran to me and gave me a huge hug. I could hear all the subtle giggles from the other girls. As I sat with the Birthday Girl while she opened all her gifts, I thought to myself, "Why me?" Why did she invite me, I'm the only boy here, why me? Then I thought, "Why not me!"

We have the same idea about God. We think to ourselves, 'God would never want to have anything to do with me'. After all, I've done too many bad things. I have a very dark past; I can't forgive myself so why should God forgive me. What we don't understand is that God doesn't see things the same way that we do. God says in His Word (The Bible) in Isaiah 55:8-9 "For my thoughts are not your thoughts neither are your ways my ways, says the LORD. For as the heavens are higher than the earth, so are my ways higher than your ways, and my thoughts than your thoughts." God knew every mistake, every sin, every choice we would make before we were born. The fact that we are alive now is proof that God has a huge plan for our future. But the first thing you must do is come to grips with the fact that God Loves You. Instead of saying 'why me'? Ignore your past, ignore the faults that you still have, ignore the pain and say "Why not me!" God made me, so of course He Loves Me! Yes, He Loves Me!

STEP TWO: Remove The Guilt

I always tell people "Guilt is a Killer"; It's like an anchor that drags you below. We try to ignore guilt. We will say, do, and come up with all sorts of new beliefs to fix our own guilt. But in the end it never goes away. I remember the first time I stole something. I was at home and my Mother left her purse on the kitchen table. I saw the opportunity to go through it to see what I could find. There was an envelope with a large amount of cash in it. At first I thought, 'what if she finds out?' But then I filled my mind with the idea 'Everybody does it' so I took a five dollar bill. Later the next day as I was walking to the store with a friend, I asked him if his Mom ever gave him any money. He said, "No, that's why I steal it from her every time I get the chance." In some strange way I felt justified for what I did. So, I kept doing it. But I knew if she ever caught me I would be in trouble. You might say, "Yeah, but you were a kid then, and kids make bad choices." But the reality of this example is that we all think like this when it comes to dealing without guilt conscience.

When we do something that we know God doesn't approve of, we just figure in our minds that 'everybody else does it', or 'this is what I am', or 'this is how God made me', and 'nobody's perfect'. We either push the blame on God so that He can't get mad at us and punish us; or we ignore the idea of the fact that there is a God and we will one day stand before Him and be held accountable for the actions and choices we've made in our lives before we leave this earth. It seems kinda scary doesn't it? Of course it would if you view God as someone who is mad at you and who is waiting to zap you into flames for all eternity when you stand before Him in judgment.

People believe that the Bible is a book about God sending all the bad people to hell, and giving all the good perfect people rules to follow, or they miss the party of eternal life with clouds and angels playing harps. So they look for a book or belief that fits their conscience. Trust me, it feels good for a while, but it will leave you empty later and spiritually bankrupt in eternity. The Bible is God's Love Letter to You; the Bible is a book of true events of people with sinful lifestyles who had God encounters and changed the world. That's what God wants to do with you. He want to use you to change the life's of other people in a good way. But first you need to see yourself for who you are; then see God for who He is. He is Love, and not some old dude sitting on the clouds in the heavens who's waiting for you to mess up so He can strike you down, He's a loving creator who Loves you and longs to have fellowship with you incessantly. In fact, He loves you so much that He paid the ultimate price, by sending His Son, Jesus Christ, in the likeness of sinful man, knowing that He would die as a ransom for all of mankind, so that whoever (this means You) wanted to come to Him could know Him, and be one with Him intimately, even as Jesus is one with Him. There is no guilt in a love story like that. So let's set that weight aside and allow God's Love to pour in, and flow freely through our hearts. God's Love is a free gift that will cost you nothing much.

STEP THREE: Accept The Gift

If it's free, then there must be some kind of trick to it; after all, nobody gives anything that's worth something of real value away for nothing. Well, that is how we think in this world. God has different plans; God is always working in our lives to give us the best. Someone once told me, "We don't know what we like, we only like what we know." I once thought Butter Pecan ice cream was my favorite, until I tried 'Bunny Tracks' ice cream for the first time. It's a silly illustration but you get the point. We will find every excuse on the planet to use to keep us from accepting/receiving God's Best. Excuses like: "The Bible was written by man, how can I trust it?", and "There are so many contradictions in the book.", or "I tried it, and it didn't work for me.", and the list goes on and on. But if we just accept it, then God will make it clear to us.

There was a guy in the Bible who was known as a rich young ruler, who knew there was a God, and he knew of God's Word. But the problem he had was that he thought he had to do something to earn eternal life.

Mark 10:17 (...there came one running, and kneeling to Him, and asked Him, Good Master, what shall I do that I may inherit eternal life?)

Gifts are given, you don't earn them. Religion on the other hand says "If you do this, then you will be good enough to get that." That, my friend, is not Love. God

51

showed us how much He loved us by giving us His only Son as a sacrificial, yet substituting payment for our sins. To so many people it sounds too good to be true, that is, that the Almighty and Only True God, because of His Great Love wherewith He loved us, would send His Only Begotten Son into a world like this to suffer and die in our place, and then go into hell itself and suffer and be tortured for the whole world, as payment for all of our sins, in order that He (Jesus) might give eternal life to as many, that is, any and every man, woman, boy or girl who would be willing to accept/receive Him (Jesus – The free gift Himself) into their heart (as their Saviour and Lord), so that He might give them eternal life and (if they allow Him) make their lives better. (***Note*** - Just because you accept Him (Jesus) into your heart, to make your life better, it doesn't mean life is going to get any easier, but you can be confident of one thing, that is, that He (Jesus) will be with you in and through any and every test and trial, and He will give you the victory, causing you to be an overcomer and more than a conqueror in this life.)

Someone once asked me, "What kind of God would do something like that for sinful, self-gratifying humans?" I responded to his question with a question of my own, asking, "What would you think of the sinful, self-gratifying person that turns down a gift like that?" He then tightened his face up and walked away. You see, under the Old Testament men had to works to fulfill God's law, as sent by God through His servant Moses; and even then, if man sinned against or transgressed God's Law, he (man) could offer up a sin offering

52

through the High Priest (God's Old Testament Preacher), and his sins or transgressions would be forgiven as a result of the shed blood of the sacrificial lamb which he would have to offer up to Him (God) to satisfy the requirement of His (God's) punishment for sins. However, because God found fault in the Law (not because the Law was unjust, but because the Law was perfect and just, and because man's imperfections were not able to keep the standards of the Law) God devised a plan' instead of continuing to offer up sin offerings for man's sins, God decided to send His Son, in the likeness of sinful flesh, to condemn sin in the flesh, by Jesus living a perfect and sinless life, and then offering up that same life as a ransom (substitute and sacrificial payment as the sinless Lamb of God who was slain for the sins of the world) for sinful and self-gratifying humans who would believe in their hearts that God Sent Jesus to die for their sins, and that God raised Jesus up from the dead as justification for Jesus' sacrifice for their sins, and then make an unashamed confession that because of what Jesus did for them, that they do make Him (Jesus) Lord of their lives, thereby imparting (giving) to them eternal life as they accept Jesus as their Saviour and Lord. That's the Good News of the New Testament Grace of God in comparison to the Old Testament Law. Under the Old Testament, anyone who rejected Moses' law died without mercy on the testimony of two or three witnesses; but under the New Testament the question is asked... Of how much worse punishment, do you suppose, will he be thought worthy who has trampled the Son of God underfoot, counted the blood of the covenant by which he was sanctified (forgiven and set apart for God's use) a common thing, and insulted the Spirit of grace (God's goodwill towards mankind, gifting man Jesus' righteousness/right- standing with God, without the works of the law, through faith, Placing upon Jesus the sins of the whole world.)?

When we being to think that we can earn God's Love, we tend to look at others as if they are either more spiritual than us, or of more value, or that they are at the same "level" we are, and that God would never want them or us. This is so not true. The Apostle Paul, a New Testament writer, wrote in the book of Romans, instructs in chapter 12 and verse 3... not to think of ourselves more highly than we ought to think, but to think soberly according as God hath dealt to every man was the measure of faith. Notice he said 'the' measure of faith, that would imply that each measure dealt to each man may be a different measure, but because he said 'the' measure of faith, that implies that the same amount of faith is given to everybody, and we all have the ability to believe for the same things with no one and no one's faith being lesser or greater than anyone else's. Please don't get it twisted, even though everyman among us receives the same measure of faith, if you choose to exercise your faith, by trusting God to meet your needs, or consulting God on a daily basis, about your life's plight, and I just decide to spit and chew bubble gum and ignore God, then it would stand to reason that by you, exercising your faith on a regular basis, that your faith is going to become more and more developed, while my faith, because of my lethargic mentality, is going to remain undeveloped or underdeveloped. So don't think that you should see either you, or anyone else on any level, but the level we develop ourselves on in faith. Besides, God values us the same. The Bible says For God so Love THE WORLD, (This means everyone) that He gave His only begotten Son, that whosoever believes in Him should not perish, but have everlasting life. (John 3:16) Have you ever presented a gift to someone only to have them reject it and walk away? What a hurtful feeling that must be. Well, that's how God feels when we continually turn down his gift of salvation, that is only found in His Son, Jesus Christ.

STEP FOUR: Let Your Pain Become Your Motivator

What moves you? What do you want to fix? Whose pain do you feel? I always tell people that the things I don't like in this world are some of the things of which I was once apart. For instance, I can't stand bullies, why? Because I spent most of my childhood being bullied. I can't stand child abuse. Why? Because I was a victim of child abuse, both physically and emotionally. These are very sensitive areas for me. I allowed these painful attacks to mold me into a bitter monster. I was told that hurt people end up hurting people.

As a kid a lot of abuse came into my life. My birth mother tossed me down a flight of steps when I was only one year old. I was taken away from her by the Department of Child Care Services. The hospital report read that I suffered from a fractured skull and both my legs were broken. I had to be fed special formulas because of malnutrition. I'm sorry to say, that it doesn't end there; before turning two years old, I was adopted into a family of people who had all sorts of dysfunctional baggage. There was no solid Godly structure in the home, nor was there any motivation of family unity. These things played a part of the emotional pain that would later take root in my life and my way of thinking. I look at the youth of today; those who cut themselves for some type of pleasure and outcry; or those who are being bullied because someone 'claims' that they are different or weak. What about the girl who paid attention to the deceptive voice that told her she wasn't as pretty as the other girls. The boy who was called fat and stupid. The child who was sexually molested and was too afraid to report it because it would bring problems in the family. Even though they kept silent, they now embrace the idea of sexual immorality as a result of the sexual violation they experienced, and the fact that they had their innocence stripped from them by someone either in the family or close to the family who told them that they loved them. These are demonic attacks which are very painful to children and adults as well.

Think about a young married couple; everything is perfect. They have a nice house. Both of them have good jobs, and they are so in love with each other, planning their future. Then one afternoon the wife comes home early to surprise her husband. As she walks into the house and heads for the living room, she hears a noise in the back room. She goes to the back to see what is going on, only to find her husband having sex with the woman who lives next door. She is crushed and overwhelmed with pain, so much so, that every time she sees a man all she remembers is the hurt she felt when she walked into that back room of her house. The pain will soon turn to areas of hate within her heart. The only thing that can cure her is the manifest presence of God's love pouring over her heart and soul, and meeting every need by way of His supernatural provision, and His divine direction. The Bible says cast your anxieties (cares) on God because He cares for you. We can't do this if we blame God for every bad thing that comes our way. However, God does give all of us the invitation to bring our problems and demonic attacks to Him and He will care for us in such a way that our pain will become our ministry. The problems we were faced with will be used as stepping stones to take us to higher levels of growth in Him, and will produce great testimonies to share with others so that they too can break free and grow.

STEP FIVE: Walk On Water

I love the story of peter jumping out of the boat and walking on the water with Jesus. Right in the middle of the storm, there is a scared, loud mouth prideful fisherman yelling from a boat, saying.. If it's really you, call me out the water to walk with you! (Matthew 14:28). Jesus called him out and Peter came out and began walking on the water. This was no magic trick, no trick of the camera, or illusion; this was an actual event (A Miracle). Does God still do miracles? Absolutely. What's the best miracle... Walking on water, or turning a stone cold street killer into a saint and lover of Jesus Christ? Or how about when the odds seem to be against you, and everyone seems to hate you, and you have nobody that believes in you, but then God turns your life around and causes you to become such a success in life that even your enemies will see it too? No matter how far you have gone into the pit of life; no matter how many bad choices you have made; God is in the water walking business. The thing that was challenging you that you thought was designed to cause you to sink and drown, God will use as a platform for you to step on, and it doesn't matter how deep the water of life gets. Just call out to Jesus and keep your eyes fixed on Him.

In this story, Peter was the one who pulled fish out of the sea, and now he's walking on top of it. What do you see yourself doing that seems impossible? If Jesus can call Peter out to walk on water, He can call you out of your boat of comfort as well. There were other disciples

59

in the boat with Peter; why did they stay in the boat and not follow Peter's lead. I would say fear. They stayed in their comfort zone. They did not want to face the unfamiliar, therefore they missed the opportunity to partake in a miracle. Go after that giant, get out of the boat, write that book, build that company, sing that song, get that education. This is how miracles are birthed.

Did you ever notice that when something good is happening for you that all sorts of problems come out of nowhere? Well, these are called storms. Remember, we have an enemy, and he is real. He will do anything he can possibly do to get you to take your eyes off of God. He manufactures storms in our lives. He is a fallen angel named Satan (the devil). He has been trying to take your soul since the day you were born. He is the one blinding the eyes of those who don't believe in God. He is the one bringing sickness and pain into the lives of those he wants to take under. He stirs up storms when we begin to walk on our miracle. When Peter started walking on the water to Jesus, the wind and waves became violent. Peter took his eyes off Jesus and put his attention on the storm and began to sink. He then yelled out, Lord Help! Jesus immediately reached in to pull him back up. (Matthew 14:30-31).

When you set your heart on your miracle, don't lose focus. Don't listen to the 'Nay Sayers'. Ignore that voice of doubt in your mind that whispers to you that you can't amount to anything. Those are lies from the enemy. Put your focus on the God whose feet were on top of the storm; not only will He call you out into your miracle, He will also keep you from sinking.

STEP SIX: Give Others The Same Gift God Has Given You

The world's system calls it "karma". It comes from a Hinduism/Buddhism belief that puts you in charge of your own fate in life. In many areas of life it is true that what you give is what you get in return. But if you base all your actions on "karma", then you have taken God out of the equation and everything begins to revolve around "self".

When we come to understand the truth that everything we have comes from God, we will come to know God in a better way. We then begin to put our dependence on God. One who is thankful is one who becomes a generous giver. I want people to know the love of God, because I want them to experience what God has planned for them. What I want for myself is what I want for others as well. I'm so thankful for the Pastor who brought me the Good news of the Gospel of Jesus Christ. That pastor shared the gift with me, and that gift has kept on giving ever since.

There are so many people hurting, so many people lost, so many people who have made a "god" of their own understanding and yet are on their way to an eternal hell. Deep down in your heart you know who Jesus is and why he died and rose on the third day. God gave us a priceless gift to show His love and forgiveness toward us. We need to embrace it and then share it. One of the greatest gifts is the gift of sharing apart of you with someone you can trust to help you. Find someone you can share your thoughts with. Tell that person about your pain. Trust me, it not only brings healing; it builds bridges with those who will encourage you and help you see things clearly.

Friend, the devil wants to make your eternal salvation complicated. The gospel is free. It is simple as A-B-C.

Admit to God that you are a sinner.
For the wages of sin is death... Romans 6;23a
Believe that the only necessary payment for your sin is Jesus' blood which He shed on the cross.
In whom we have redemption through his blood, the forgiveness of sins, according to the riches of his grace. Ephesians 1:7
Confess to Him your need to be saved.
For whosoever shall call upon the name of the Lord shall be saved. Romans 10:13
Once you are saved, read His word, the Holy Bible, to gain assurance that you will never go to hell.
He that believeth on the Son hath everlasting life... John 3:36a

If you would like to be saved from hell right now, you can ask the Lord in a prayer just like this, to know you are saved. "Lord Jesus, I know I am a sinner on my way to hell. Please save me and make me your child. I thank you for shedding your blood for me. In Jesus' name, Amen."

Please understand reciting these words is not what saves you, but trusting the shed blood of Jesus alone to save your soul.

Made in the USA
Monee, IL
25 March 2021